READ
REFLECT
RESPOND

Comprehension Skill-Boosters

by JANICE GREENE

Comprehension Skill-Boosters

Development and Production: Laurel Associates, Inc.
Cover Design: Image Quest, Inc.

SADDLEBACK
EDUCATIONAL PUBLISHING
Three Watson
Irvine, CA 92618-2767
Website: www.sdlback.com

ISBN 1-59905-002-1

Printed in the United States of America
12 11 10 09 08 07 06   9 8 7 6 5 4 3 2 1

READ · REFLECT · RESPOND
CONTENTS

RESPOND: *Circle a letter or word, fill in the blanks, or write out the answer.*

Build your vocabulary.

1. Someone who is *sleep deprived* is
   a. not getting enough sleep.
   b. getting too much sleep.
   c. sick from the bite of the tsetse fly.

2. Someone who is *paranoid*
   a. places too much trust in others.
   b. is unreasonably suspicious of others.
   c. has no interest in others.

3. *Insomniacs* are people who
   a. dream too much.
   b. hardly move during sleep.
   c. have trouble sleeping.

4. If something is *beneficial*, it is
   a. harmful.
   b. good for you.
   c. superficial.

Recall details.

5. How often do people dream in a night?

   _____

6. How long do dreams last?

   _____

7. Circle three things that happen during sleep.

heart slows down	fingers twitch
hair stops growing	muscles relax
breathing slows down	eyes roll back

8. Sleepers normally change position about (58 / 5 / 30) times a night.

9. Afternoon naps are (lazy / beneficial / unhealthy).

Summarize.

10. After a sleepless night, your state of mind would be _____

    _____

    _____

Draw conclusions.

11. If you're sleep deprived, it's
    a. not safe to watch TV.
    b. not smart to drive a vehicle.
    c. probably good for you.

12. If you've gone several days without sleep, you might think
    a. everyone's plotting against you.
    b. sleeping is a waste of time.
    c. you're having an enjoyable, productive day.

13. While sleeping, you probably wouldn't
    a. change your position.
    b. notice someone in the room.
    c. hear a very loud noise.

Look it up in a reference source.

14. What is sleep apnea?

    _____

    _____

    _____

READ: *Queen Mary led a full but tragic life.*

MARY, QUEEN OF SCOTS

Born in 1542, Mary became the queen of Scotland before she was one week old. At age five, she was sent to France to attend school. At 15, she married the French crown prince. Soon after the marriage, the prince became Francis II, King of France. Unfortunately, he died only 17 months later.

In 1561, Mary, raised a loyal Roman Catholic, returned to Scotland. She found that Scotland was becoming a Protestant country. She married her Catholic cousin, Henry Stewart, who was known as Lord Darnley. The marriage alarmed powerful Protestant leaders. They revolted against Mary and Lord Darnley. But Mary, who joined her soldiers on the battlefield, stopped the revolt quickly.

In 1567, Lord Darnley was murdered. Most people believed the Earl of Bothwell, a great favorite of Mary's, was behind the murder. Three months after Darnley was killed, Mary married Bothwell. Outraged, the Scottish nobles turned against her. She raised an army against them, but her soldiers were defeated. Mary was forced to step down from the throne and was sent to prison. Her son, James VI, who was only a baby, was crowned king.

With the help of a few brave friends, Mary escaped from prison. She rallied a large force behind her and, once again, engaged the Scottish nobles in battle. But again, she was defeated. At this point Mary decided to leave Scotland. She went to England to beg support from her cousin, Queen Elizabeth I.

Elizabeth was not happy to see Mary—who was next in line for the throne of England. She feared that Mary would try to overthrow her. Instead of helping her, Elizabeth had her imprisoned.

Mary spent the next 19 years in prison. Then she was implicated in a plot to assassinate Elizabeth. On February 8, 1587, Elizabeth had Mary beheaded.

REFLECT: *Think about leading a country.*

1. In Mary's time, a country's leader was determined by *birth*. Many modern countries choose their leaders by *election*. Which method do you think is best? Why?

_____

_____

2. List two changes you would like to make if you were the leader of your country.

- _____
- _____

RESPOND: *Circle a letter or word, fill in the blanks, or write out the answer.*

Build your vocabulary.

overthrow	outraged	alarmed
revolt	implicate	rally

1. When people are extremely angry, they're _____.

2. People _____ when they rise up against established authority.

3. To _____ a government is to take away its power.

4. To _____ a group of people is to gather them together for a common purpose.

5. Another word for *frightened* is _____.

6. To _____ someone is to imply involvement.

Recall details.

7. How many times did Mary marry? _____

8. How many people were murdered? _____

9. Which two people were Mary's cousins?
   a. Francis II   c. Bothwell
   b. Elizabeth I   d. Darnley

Put details in order.

10. Number the events to show the order in which they happened.

    ____ Mary is forced to step down from her throne.

    ____ Darnley is killed, probably by Bothwell.

    ____ Mary's French husband, Francis II, dies.

    ____ Mary escapes prison and flees to England.

    ____ Elizabeth I has Mary beheaded.

    ____ Mary marries Lord Darnley.

Draw conclusions.

11. Circle three words that could describe Mary.

timid	religious	bold
determined	fearful	victorious

Look it up in a reference source.

12. Who was James Stuart, Earl of Moray?

    _____
    _____
    _____

13. How did Darnley die?

    _____
    _____
    _____

READ: Want to create your own video games? Take a class!

GAMING 101

Did you know that you can study video gaming in colleges across the country? Courses offered include animation, game development, and computer music. At least 50 U.S. colleges offer courses in video games.

Do you want to be a developer or designer? The University of Washington offers a certificate in game design. At the University of Pennsylvania, you can get a master's degree in computer graphics and game technology. Students from schools like these will supply a growing demand for game developers. The video game industry is booming! That's why video game companies are hungry for new workers with new ideas. They need the skills and tastes of young people who've grown up with video games.

Jason Della Rocca is executive director of the International Game Developers Association. He says that in the early days of gaming, one developer could teach a handful of workers what to do. Back then, that was just about all

http://www.cis.upenn.edu/grad/cggt/cggt-overview.shtml

Penn
UNIVERSITY *of* PENNSYLVANIA

MASTER OF SCIENCE IN ENGINEERING IN COMPUTER GRAPHICS AND GAME TECHNOLOGY

CGGT HOME — ADMISSIONS — CORE AREAS OF STUDY

DEGREE REQUIREMENTS — SUBMATRICULATION — CONTACT US

Interactive entertainment and computer-animated visual effects are now part of our mainstream culture.

a company needed to develop new games. Today, game design is more complicated. The development of one game can cost $10 million and require 200 workers! Companies have *many* positions to fill.

Some people don't see video games as a serious subject. They feel that courses on video games shouldn't be taught in college. But many colleges insist that the gaming industry needs technically proficient workers. And one of a university's jobs is to supply what the working world needs.

REFLECT: Think about video games and movies.

How are movies and video games similar? How are they different?

SIMILAR: _____   DIFFERENT: _____

_____   _____

_____   _____

_____   _____

_____   _____

RESPOND: *Circle a letter or word, fill in the blanks, or write out the answer.*

Build your vocabulary.

1. What is *technology*?
   a. using science for practical purposes
   b. manufacturing machines to make goods
   c. programming computers in colleges

2. What is a *design*?
   a. a painting or drawing in a book
   b. fancy lettering and artwork
   c. a drawing or plan to serve as a guide

3. *Animation* is the process of
   a. making drawings that move.
   b. creating different moves for video characters.
   c. drawing on computers.

4. A *certificate* is
   a. an application for a job.
   b. written proof of something.
   c. a doctor's prescription.

5. The video game industry is *booming*.
   a. falling apart
   b. growing quickly
   c. losing money

6. Companies are *hungry* for new workers.
   a. eager   b. open   c. not ready

7. One developer could teach a *handful* of workers.
   a. five   b. a lot   c. a few

Fact or opinion? Write F or O.

8. ____ Video games aren't a serious subject to study in college.

9. ____ At least 50 colleges offer courses in video games.

10. ____ Developing a single game might require 200 workers.

11. ____ Supplying new workers is a college's main job.

Identify the main ideas.

12. What *two* main points does the author make?
    a. The University of Pennsylvania offers a master's degree in gaming.
    b. Many colleges offer courses in video game development.
    c. The video game industry needs many new workers.
    d. Colleges should not offer courses in video gaming.

Draw a conclusion.

13. Why do companies need the skills and tastes of young people?

    _____

    _____

    _____

    _____

Look it up in a reference source.

14. List several jobs/careers available in the video game development industry.

    _____

    _____

    _____

READ: *Some facts about that red stuff in a bottle.*

KETCHUP

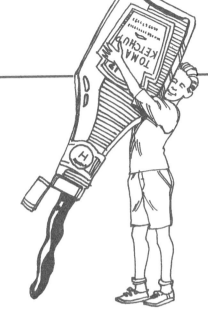

The first ketchup wasn't made of tomatoes. *Ke-tsiap* was invented by the Chinese in the 1690s. It was a sauce made of pickled fish and spices. European explorers discovered *ke-tsiap* in Malaysia.

The red sauce we now call ketchup first became popular in England. Its popularity quickly spread to the American colonies.

Ketchup wasn't made with tomatoes until the 1700s. Why? Until then, people thought those bright red globes were poisonous! Tomatoes are related to the belladonna and nightshade plants—both toxic. Many people believed that tomatoes weren't safe to eat. Thomas Jefferson, though, loved tomatoes. Eventually other bold folks tried them, too. Seeing that tomatoes didn't kill anyone, more and more people began to enjoy them. Today, of course, tomatoes are the main ingredient in ketchup.

In the 1700s, Americans loved ketchup —but it was a pain in the neck to make. When first mixed up together, the ingredients were very thin and watery. Ketchup had to be boiled for hours to become thick. It also had to be stirred constantly so it wouldn't burn. In 1875, Henry J. Heinz came to the rescue with bottled ketchup. "Precooked ketchup," he said, "is a blessed relief for Mother and the other women in the household." More than half of the ketchup sold in the United States today is made by the H. J. Heinz Company.

REFLECT: *Think about ketchup and other condiments.*

1. Ketchup is a *condiment*—something used to enhance the flavor of food. Circle nine items below that are also condiments.

lettuce	soy sauce	tartar sauce	salsa	hot dogs
pickle relish	mustard	ice cream	tortilla chips	milk
mayonnaise	horseradish	honey	wheat bread	chutney

2. What is your favorite condiment? _____

RESPOND: *Circle a letter or word, fill in the blanks, or write out the answer.*

Recall details.

1. The first ketchup (*ke-tsiap*) was
   a. a thin and watery liquid.
   b. unsafe for people to eat.
   c. made from fish and spices.

2. Tomatoes are
   a. related to poisonous plants.
   b. poisonous only when cooked.
   c. poisonous when eaten raw.

3. Making homemade ketchup requires
   a. using precooked tomatoes.
   b. adding Henry J. Heinz's spices.
   c. long hours of boiling and stirring.

Recognize the author's tone.

4. The *tone* of the reading is
   a. light and informal.
   b. formal and serious.
   c. scientific and scholarly.

Put details in order.

5. Number the events to show the order in which they happened.

   ____ Americans spent hours making homemade ketchup.

   ____ *Ke-tsiap*, made of fish and spices, was invented.

   ____ Ketchup became popular in the colonies.

   ____ Ketchup became popular in England.

   ____ Henry J. Heinz began selling bottled ketchup.

Fact or opinion? Write F or O.

6. ____ Everyone hated making homemade ketchup.

7. ____ People once thought that tomatoes were unsafe to eat.

Make comparisons.

8. Explain two differences between *ke-tsiap* and the ketchup sold in the United States today.

   • _____

   _____

   • _____

   • _____

Draw conclusions.

9. An ad claimed that bottled ketchup was "a blessed relief for Mother and the other women in the household." What does this suggest about the *men* in the household?

   _____

   _____

Look it up in a reference source.

10. After ketchup, what is the most popular condiment in North America?

    _____

11. Read the label on a bottle of ketchup or another condiment. List the ingredients. Write the main ingredients on the lines below. Hint: The main ingredient is listed first.

    _____

    _____

    _____

    _____

READ: *The story of a gang-fighter.*

ELIOT NESS

In 1929, Prohibition was the law in the United States. That means it was illegal to make or sell liquor. Many people drank anyway—but illegal liquor was expensive. Lured by money, gangs got into the business of making and selling liquor. Rival gangs fought bloody battles over the control of markets. Of all the gangsters, the most famous was Al Capone of Chicago.

The Justice Department formed a 15-man team to go after the gangs. They came to be called the "Untouchables," because they could not be bribed. Their leader was Eliot Ness.

In a few months, Ness's team raided dozens of alcohol-making operations. In a few short years, Ness reduced crime substantially. He shut down most of Al Capone's liquor-making operations and helped put him behind bars. Amazingly, Ness never fired a single shot while on duty.

Prohibition ended in 1933. Ness moved to Cleveland, Ohio, where he became the head of public safety. He cleaned up widespread corruption in the police department. Dozens of gang members were brought to trial.

Eliot Ness was not so successful in his personal life. One night after a party, he skidded on an icy street and hit another car. No one was seriously injured, so Ness went home. But the other driver recognized his license plate, EN-1. He reported Ness to the police, and the accident made the newspaper headlines. It was reported that Ness had been driving drunk. Ness insisted he hadn't been drinking, but the next day he resigned.

After that, Ness's life went downhill. He tried his luck with several new businesses, but all of them failed. The great crime fighter had no talent for making money. He died at the age of 54, several thousand dollars in debt.

REFLECT: *Think about gangs and laws.*

1. What is one way that criminal gangs make money today?

_____

_____

_____

_____

2. During Prohibition, liquor was illegal. Name three activities or substances that are illegal today.

- _____

- _____

- _____

R̶E̶S̶P̶O̶N̶D: *Circle a letter or word, fill in the blanks, or write out the answer.*

Build your vocabulary.

1. Gangs were *lured* by the prospect of money.
   a. snagged
   b. caught
   c. attracted

2. Ness cut down on crime *substantially*.
   a. quite a lot
   b. superficially
   c. somewhat

3. The police department was very *corrupt*.
   a. strong, powerful
   b. inefficient, clumsy
   c. dishonest, untrustworthy

4. Ness cut down on *juvenile* crime.
   a. committed against young people
   b. committed by young people
   c. childish pranks

5. Ness *resigned* from his job.
   a. quit
   b. took a pay cut
   c. retired

6. *Rival* gangs battled over territory.
   a. competing
   b. neighborhood
   c. bloodthirsty

Recall details.

7. Circle three periods of Ness's life that are described in the reading.

   He helped put Capone behind bars.

   He tried his luck with several businesses.

   He was the leader of the "Untouchables."

   He cut down on Cleveland's juvenile crime.

   He was Cleveland's head of public safety.

   He tried to capture a serial killer.

Draw conclusions.

8. Why did the Justice Department demand men who were *untouchable*?
   a. They wanted top-performing police officers.
   b. Police had accepted bribes in the past.
   c. They wanted men who kept to themselves.

9. Why did Ness resign from his job after the car accident?
   a. He'd been seriously injured.
   b. He'd failed at his business.
   c. His reputation had been damaged.

Look it up in a reference source.

10. What is a *speakeasy*?

    _____

    _____

11. What did *bootleggers* do?

    _____

    _____

READ: *This device makes fast food even faster!*

HYPERACTIVE BOB

Imagine pulling into a fast-food restaurant parking lot. As you park, a camera on the roof zooms in on your car. A computer compares your car to other cars of the same shape and size. The computer's memory stores orders from people with cars like yours. Based on those past orders, the computer decides what you probably want to eat. Your order flashes on the screen. By the time you've entered the restaurant, your food is being cooked.

Sound farfetched? A simpler version of this technology is already being used. Its name? HyperActive Bob. Right now, HyperActive Bob is used in many restaurants to show workers how many customers are coming.

HyperActive Bob helps solve fast-food restaurants' biggest headache. Think about it. Cooks are never sure how many people are going to show up, or what they'll order. Fast food isn't fast unless it's cooked *before* the customer

shows up. If cooks grill too few burgers, customers end up waiting. If they grill too many, a lot of burgers may end up in the trash.

"Bob" instantly alerts workers as new customers arrive. Restaurants like using the system. Much less food is wasted. Cooks and other employees find that Bob takes a lot of stress out of their jobs. Waiting times for customers have been cut by a minute or more. And, as they say in business, "time is money"!

REFLECT: *Think about fast-food restaurants and other businesses.*

1. For what purpose are cameras *usually* used in businesses?

   _____

2. Recently, fast-food restaurants have put less-fattening items on their menus. Name two of those items.

   • _____

   • _____

3. How would you feel about having a camera recording all of your daily activities?

   _____

   _____

   _____

   _____

RESPOND: *Circle a letter or word, fill in the blanks, or write out the answer.*

Build your vocabulary.

1. A *farfetched* idea
   a. comes from a distant place.
   b. is hard to understand.
   c. isn't based on clear thinking.

2. A simpler *version* is a
   a. particular form of something.
   b. machine with fewer parts.
   c. rough draft of something.

3. Some synonyms for *stress* are
   a. worry, concern, fear.
   b. strain, pressure, tension.
   c. anger, fury, rage.

4. A computer's *memory* is the
   a. design of the keyboard.
   b. ability to produce graphics.
   c. amount of stored information.

Draw conclusions.

5. Compared to a sports car, a minivan at the drive-up window means
   a. a bigger food order.
   b. disagreements about what to order.
   c. a customer with less money to spend.

6. If customers wait a long time for fast food, they might
   a. end up ordering more food.
   b. go somewhere else next time.
   c. order less food next time.

7. When employees' jobs are less stressful, they will
   a. eat more while on the job.
   b. deserve more money.
   c. be less likely to quit.

8. The phrase "time is money" means
   a. people lose money if they work too fast.
   b. the less time you work, the less you earn.
   c. the quicker the sale, the more you can sell.

Recall details.

9. HyperActive Bob is the name of a (fast employee / computer system).

10. Fast food must be cooked (before / after) the customer arrives.

11. If restaurants make too little food, people end up (waiting / dieting).

12. A simple version of HyperActive Bob is being (developed / used).

13. It can be (stressful / wasteful) for a cook to get too many orders at once.

14. HyperActive Bob records people (coming to / leaving) a restaurant.

Look it up in a reference source.

15. "The Pig Stand" was the first drive-in restaurant. Where and in what year was it opened?

WHERE? _____

WHAT YEAR? _____

READ: *These ovens cook food from the inside out.*

THE AMAZING MICROWAVE

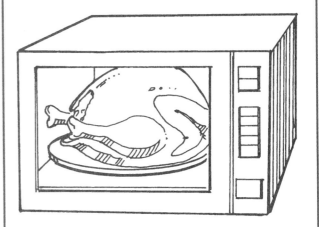

Before there were microwave ovens, food was always heated from the *outside*. Think, for example, of how a turkey is cooked in a regular oven. The heat must travel from the skin all the way into the middle of the body. In contrast, microwave ovens cook food from the *inside* out.

Many foods are mostly made of water and fats—which are made of *molecules*. These are tiny particles that can only be seen through a microscope. Molecules are charged with electricity. A *positive* charge is at one end of each molecule. At the other end is a *negative* charge.

Each charge pulls toward its *opposite*. Negative charges pull toward positive charges, and positive charges pull toward negative charges. This is how the molecules line up: positive to negative and negative to positive. A turkey is made up of countless molecules, all lined up with each other.

When a microwave hits a molecule, a change takes place. The molecule *turns* until its charge lines up with the charge of the microwave.

Inside the oven, microwaves bounce around at an amazing speed. They change directions millions of times per second. The molecules in the turkey turn around at the same great speed. Those zooming molecules create friction—the energy produced when objects rub against each other. Friction creates heat. It's that heat that cooks the turkey—from the inside out.

REFLECT: *Think about the food we eat.*

1. Name two precooked foods that are sold in packages.

   - _____
   - _____

2. Name two foods that are usually eaten raw.

   - _____
   - _____

3. List three foods you would usually heat or cook . . .

   in a microwave:

   - _____
   - _____

   in a regular oven:

   - _____

RESPOND: *Circle a letter or word, fill in the blanks, or write out the answer.*

Recall details. *(Write **T** for true or **F** for false.)*

1. _____ Most foods we eat are full of water and fats.

2. _____ Regular ovens cook food from the inside out.

3. _____ When hit by microwaves, molecules quickly melt.

4. _____ Molecules are charged with electricity.

5. _____ Molecules moving at great speed create friction.

6. _____ A molecule has a different charge at each end.

7. _____ Friction creates light, which cooks our food.

8. _____ Positive charges line up with negative charges.

Write out the answer.

9. How does a regular oven bake a pie?

   _____

   _____

10. What happens to molecules when they're hit by a microwave?

    _____

    _____

    _____

11. What causes friction?

    _____

    _____

    _____

12. How do molecules line up?

    _____

    _____

    _____

    _____

Build your vocabulary.

13. *Molecules* are (telepathic / microscopic).

14. To *contrast* two things is to point out the (differences / similarities).

Draw a conclusion.

15. Soup heated in a microwave is very hot. But the cup that holds the soup is cool enough to hold. Why? (Hint: What's the difference between a cup and food?)

    _____

    _____

    _____

    _____

    _____

    _____

    _____

Look it up in a reference source.

16. The milk we buy has been pre-heated. Why?

    _____

    _____

    _____

    _____

    _____

READ: *What was it like to hunt the largest animal on earth?*

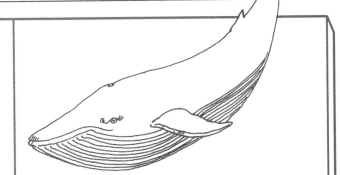

WHALE HUNTING: _____

The year: 1821. The place: 200 miles off the coast of New England. For months you've been searching for whales. Now, suddenly, a man shouts, "There she blows!"

Everyone is excited. Your ship heads toward the whale. The crew gets the whaleboats ready to go. Harpoons are sharpened one last time.

Now your ship is a mile from the whale. Moving the mainsail, the crew brings the ship to a near standstill. Using ropes, the crew lowers the five whaleboats into the water. Then they race after the whale, rowing as fast as they can.

Your boat reaches the whale first. You can hear the hollow, wet roar of the whale's breath. The whale's eye is only 12 feet away! The harpooner raises his weapon—and throws. The harpoon, attached to the boat with a rope, sinks into the whale's body. Suddenly, the giant turns into an angry, panicked monster. It could easily kill a man with a flick of its huge tail. Luckily, the whale speeds away, pulling the boat with it.

Your whale boat bounces along the tops of the waves.

Eventually, the whale wears itself out. Slowly, the crew hauls in the rope. The boat comes closer and closer to the beast. Then one of the men takes up a killing lance. The weapon is 12 feet long, with a petal-shaped blade. The man stabs the whale again and again. Finally, the mammoth animal dies, and the water turns red.

The exhausted men pull the 60-ton body back to the ship. They tie the whale to the side of the ship. Then a wooden plank is lowered for the men to stand on. Standing next to the whale, they begin to rip the blubber from its body. Back on shore, the blubber will be boiled into oil, and this oil will light the lamps of our nation.

REFLECT: *Think about hunting whales, whale oil, and other sources of energy.*

1. Write an interesting subtitle for the reading on the line above the article.

2. Do you think you would have enjoyed hunting whales? Why or why not?

   _____

3. Whale oil was an important source of energy in 1821. Name two sources of energy that are used today.

   • _____   • _____

RESPOND: *Circle a letter or word, fill in the blanks, or write out the answer.*

Identify synonyms.

1. The ship is almost at a *standstill*.

   (stop / barrier)

2. The whale becomes *panicked*.

   (vicious / frightened)

3. A *flick* of its tail can be deadly.

   (snap / snip)

4. *Eventually*, the whale tires out.

   (finally / soon)

5. The whale is killed with a *lance*.

   (pole / spear)

6. The men stand on a wooden *plank*.

   (board / mast)

7. The *blubber* is ripped from the whale's body.

   (fat / skin)

Draw conclusions. (Some questions have more than one answer.)

8. On every whaling ship there are
   a. two small motors.
   b. several whaleboats.
   c. many harpoons.

9. *"There she blows!"* means
   a. "I see a whale."
   b. "The wind is blowing."
   c. "Look at that boat!"

10. If the rope attached to the harpoon breaks,
    a. the whale might attack the boat.
    b. the whale would get away.
    c. the hunt is over.

11. What might attract men to hunting whales?
    a. love of adventure
    b. love of machinery
    c. love of the sea

12. To hunt whales, it helps to be
    a. brave.
    b. lucky.
    c. indecisive.

13. The whale hunters are 200 miles off the coast of New England. Their whaling ship is in what body of water?
    a. Red Sea
    b. Puget Sound
    c. Atlantic Ocean

Look it up in a reference source.

14. Herman Melville wrote a famous novel about whale-hunting. What is the name of that novel? When was it published?

    NAME OF NOVEL: _____

    _____

    YEAR PUBLISHED: _____

READ: *He vowed that the world would remember the Holocaust.*

SIMON WIESENTHAL: NAZI HUNTER

Simon Wiesenthal had three narrow brushes with death. In 1941, German soldiers rounded up a group of Jews, including Wiesenthal. An officer began shooting them, one by one. As the shooter approached Wiesenthal, church bells rang. "Enough!" the officer cried out. It was time to go to church.

That year, the Nazis began what they called their "final solution." That meant sending Jews to concentration camps to die. Wiesenthal himself lost 89 members of his family. Like them, he, too, was sent to a concentration camp. He had little hope of surviving. Twice, he tried to commit suicide. Then he had a conversation with a Nazi soldier. The soldier bet him that no one would ever believe what happened in the concentration camps. The remark gave Wiesenthal the will to live. He vowed to make sure that the whole world knew what happened in the camps.

In May 1945, American soldiers freed the prisoners in the camps. They had turned into living skeletons. Wiesenthal, who was six feet tall, weighed only 97 pounds. He was too weak to stand.

Soon after he was freed, Wiesenthal started the job that would last the rest of his life. He began collecting evidence about what the Nazis had done. After the war, Nazis fled from Germany. They settled in many different countries, including the United States. They changed their names and began new lives. But Wiesenthal hunted down hundreds of them. He brought them to trial for their terrible crimes. He was called the "deputy for the dead."

Most of all, Wiesenthal helped keep the memory of the Holocaust alive. When people wanted to forget about it, he reminded them. He once said, "When we come to the other world and meet the millions of Jews who died in the camps . . . I will say, 'I didn't forget you.'" Born in 1908, Simon Wiesenthal died September 21, 2005. He was 96.

For the dead and the living we must bear witness

**UNITED STATES
HOLOCAUST MEMORIAL MUSEUM**

REFLECT: *Think about wars.*

1. Would you volunteer to fight in a war? Why or why not?

_____

_____

_____

_____

2. Some people claim that the Holocaust never happened. Imagine that you are Simon Wiesenthal. What would you tell these people?

_____

_____

_____

RESPOND: *Circle a letter or word, fill in the blanks, or write out the answer.*

Interpret figurative language.

1. He had a *narrow brush with death*.
   a. came close to dying
   b. dreamed of dying
   c. was saved by a doctor

2. The prisoners were *living skeletons*.
   a. looked as spooky as skeletons
   b. were so thin you could see their bones
   c. had no skin

3. Wiesenthal was a *deputy for the dead*.
   a. brought the Nazis to justice
   b. was deputized by the Nazis
   c. searched for the missing dead

4. What does it mean to *keep a memory alive*?
   a. mentally relive it
   b. make a movie about it
   c. keep talking about it

Draw a conclusion.

5. A soldier stopped shooting Jews because it was time to go to church. This was weird because
   a. the soldier still had bullets.
   b. in the soldier's religion, it's a sin to kill people.
   c. most soldiers don't go to church services.

Make inferences.

6. The author of the reading
   a. is not impressed with Wiesenthal.
   b. admires Wiesenthal.
   c. pities Wiesenthal for his hard life.

7. Wiesenthal found *the will to live*.
   a. a will that he had written
   b. inner strength to keep living
   c. got enough food

Recall details. (Write **T** for true or **F** for false.)

8. ____ The "final solution" meant sending the Jews to the U.S.

9. ____ Wiesenthal worked to keep the memory of the Holocaust alive.

10. ____ Ninety-eight members of Wiesenthal's family were killed.

Look it up in a reference source.

11. Whom did the Nazis kill besides Jews?

_____

_____

_____

_____

READ: *A seesaw is a type of simple machine.*

SEESAW SCIENCE

A seesaw or teeter-totter is a *lever*. A lever is a simple machine that uses little energy to lift objects. A smaller person can lift a much larger one on a seesaw.

The main part of a seesaw is a board attached to a metal pipe called a *fulcrum*. The fulcrum supports the board.

Here's what happens when someone sits at one end of the seesaw. That person's weight provides the *force* to lift the person on the other end.

If both people weigh the same, the force is equal. That means the board will balance. If one person is heavier than the other, the board will not balance. The heavier person will sink to the ground.

To balance the board, the force must be even. There are two ways to do this. First, the heavier person could move closer to the fulcrum. Or, the fulcrum itself could be moved.

Suppose a 200-pound person and a 100-pound person sit on a seesaw. The 200-pound person weighs twice as much as the 100-pound person. How can the board be balanced? The 200-pound person must sit *twice as close* to the fulcrum as the 100-pound person.

There are many types of levers. A *wheelbarrow* is a different kind of lever than a seesaw. In a wheelbarrow, the fulcrum is the wheel. The weight, or load, is between the fulcrum and the force. The force is the person lifting the wheelbarrow handles.

REFLECT: *Think about the machines around you.*

1. Name five simple machines that help you work in your home.

   - _____
   - _____
   - _____
   - _____
   - _____

2. Circle four machines that require constant energy from you to keep operating.

dishwasher	scissors
hand saw	food processor
shovel	potato peeler
electric fan	clothes dryer

RESPOND: *Circle a letter or word, fill in the blanks, or write out the answer.*

Make inferences.

1. Circle three examples of *levers*.

   dolly   corkscrew

   axe   hammer

   crowbar   ice cream scoop

2. Is a screwdriver a lever? _____

   Does a screwdriver become a lever when it's used to lift the lid off a can of paint? _____

Build your vocabulary.

3. A *f*_ _ _ _ is any push or pull on an object.

4. A *f*_ _ _ _ _ _ is the support on which a lever rests.

5. A *m*_ _ _ _ _ _ _ is any device that can change the speed, direction, or amount of a force.

6. A *l*_ _ _ _ is a simple machine made of a bar that turns on a support.

Recall details. (Write **T** for true or **F** for false.)

7. ____ A lightweight person can lift a heavy person on a seesaw.

8. ____ To balance a seesaw, the weight must be the same at both ends.

9. ____ The fulcrum of the wheelbarrow is its long handles.

10. ____ A wheelbarrow is one of many simple machines we use.

11. ____ The part of the lever that supports it is called the "load."

12. ____ Unless both people weigh the same, a seesaw can't move.

13. ____ A seesaw cannot be balanced by moving the fulcrum.

14. ____ A seesaw can be balanced if the heavier person moves closer to the fulcrum.

Match synonyms.

repositioned   hoisted   equal   kind

15. even / _____

16. lifted / _____

17. type / _____

18. moved / _____

Look it up in a reference source.

19. Name three other simple machines.
   - _____
   - _____
   - _____

20. Who invented the "assembly line" approach to car manufacturing?

   _____

READ: *A few stories you may not know about some past presidents.*

LITTLE-KNOWN FACTS ABOUT OUR PRESIDENTS

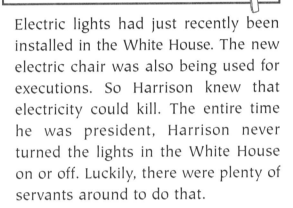

WARREN G. HARDING'S BELOVED AIREDALE TERRIER, LADDIE BOY, HAD HIS OWN CHAIR AT CABINET MEETINGS.

- **James Madison was president from 1809 to 1817.** Like every president, he was commander in chief of the military. But James Madison actually *led* troops. During the war of 1812, the British attacked Washington, D.C. Quick to respond, President Madison took charge of an artillery battery. But when American troops gathered, Madison didn't stick around. He left the city quickly.

- **John Quincy Adams was president from 1825 to 1829.** In hot weather, he'd go for a swim in the Potomac River —without a swimsuit. One morning, Adams was swimming when a reporter came by. Her name was Anne Royall. She'd been trying to interview the president for weeks. This time she quietly sneaked up on him—and sat on his clothes! She told Adams she wouldn't leave without an interview. So Adams became the first—and as far as we know, the only—president to be interviewed in the nude.

- **Benjamin Harrison was president from 1889 to 1893.** Strange to say, Harrison was afraid of electricity!

Electric lights had just recently been installed in the White House. The new electric chair was also being used for executions. So Harrison knew that electricity could kill. The entire time he was president, Harrison never turned the lights in the White House on or off. Luckily, there were plenty of servants around to do that.

- **Warren G. Harding was president from 1921 to 1923.** Like all presidents, he had the power to pardon people who were about to be executed. But President Harding, who loved animals, pardoned a dog. He'd read that a dog in Pennsylvania was about to be put to death. Why? The animal had been brought into the United States illegally, so officials had decided to destroy it. Harding wrote a letter to the governor of Pennsylvania. The governor made sure that the dog's life was spared.

REFLECT: *Think about our country's presidents.*

1. Name any three presidents who are *not* mentioned in the reading.

   - _____
   - _____
   - _____

2. Name one fact about one of our U.S. presidents.

   _____
   _____
   _____

RESPOND: *Circle a letter or word, fill in the blanks, or write out the answer.*

Use context clues.

1. A *commander-in-chief* is
   a. the top leader of the military.
   b. chief of all Native Americans.
   c. head of the State Department.

2. *Executed* means
   a. saved from death by a pardon.
   b. living in the United States illegally.
   c. put to death as a legal punishment.

3. Someone who receives a *pardon* is
   a. excused without any punishment.
   b. imprisoned as punishment.
   c. forced to apologize.

4. To *spare* people is to
   a. allow them to stay in the country.
   b. prevent them from being punished.
   c. charge them only a fine.

Recall details.

5. Who was president during the War of 1812?
   a. Harding   b. Madison   c. Adams

6. The electric chair became a common form of execution when
   a. Harrison was president.
   b. Adams was president.
   c. Madison was president.

7. What *two* presidential powers were mentioned in the reading?
   a. power over the military
   b. power over the Internet
   c. power to pardon people

8. President Harding communicated with the governor of Pennsylvania by
   a. calling him on the phone.
   b. writing him a letter.
   c. sending him an e-mail.

Draw conclusions.

9. Why did Anne Royall sit on President Adams' clothes?
   a. to keep them warm for him
   b. to play a harmless trick
   c. to keep him from dressing and leaving

10. Why was President Harrison afraid of electricity?
    a. He was afraid of many things.
    b. The wiring in the White House was unsafe.
    c. He didn't trust this new invention.

11. Why couldn't a president lead troops into battle today?
    a. We'd never allow the president to be exposed to danger.
    b. His wife wouldn't permit it.
    c. It's forbidden by the Constitution.

Look it up in a reference source.

12. Who was the first president born in the 20th century?

_____

READ: *Express yourself—with a car.*

CARS WITH "FEELINGS"

Can you believe it? Someday you may be able to drive an "expressive" car—one that shows *your* feelings. It's true. Four Japanese engineers have designed a car that conveys "emotions."

The car uses hood designs that light up to show moods ranging from happy to sad. The designs have several colors: yellow is happy, blue is sad, and red is angry. The hood designs resemble faces. They have eyebrows and eyes that even shed "tears."

Here's how it works: Suppose another driver swerves in front of you. You take your foot off the gas and press down on the brakes. As you quickly steer out of the other car's way, the emotional car records all these actions.

HAPPY (YELLOW)   **SAD** (DARK BLUE)

TIRED (LIGHT BLUE)   **ANGRY** (RED)

It responds with a very "angry" look. Now the headlights appear to be slanted at a 45-degree angle. The "eyebrow" lights slope downward, as if the car is frowning. All the hood lights glow red. Flashing "angry lights" at a careless driver is supposed to make you feel better.

Engineers say their invention enables you to express yourself through your car. Some people argue we're already close enough to our cars. Do you think it's a good idea to let other drivers know how we feel? Maybe a car that "frowns" and shows "tears" really is the way to go. Or maybe we don't really need "angry lights" to show other drivers what we think of them. What's your opinion?

REFLECT: *Think about cars and their owners.*

1. In your opinion, what's the worst driving habit a person can have?

   _____

2. How do people show their personality through their cars? Give several examples.

   _____

   _____

3. How do you think you would react to an "angry" car driving behind you?

   _____

   _____

RESPOND: *Circle a letter or word, fill in the blanks, or write out the answer.*

Build your vocabulary.

1. Something that's *expressive* is
   a. extremely fast-moving.
   b. full of meaning or feeling.
   c. always angry or sad.

2. A driver who *swerves*
   a. jumps ahead quickly.
   b. deliberately tries to hit you.
   c. suddenly turns to one side.

3. Headlights that *resemble* angry eyes
   a. look like angry eyes.
   b. are extremely large.
   c. glow like hot coals.

4. Something that *slopes* is
   a. upright.
   b. slanted.
   c. flat.

Identify the author's attitude.

5. The author of the reading feels that "expressive" cars
   a. would cost too much.
   b. are a fanciful idea.
   c. are badly needed.

Identify emotions. *(Circle four examples.)*

6. determination   surprise
   resentment   intelligence
   belief   joy
   fear   fatigue

Give an example.

7. When might you want to flash another driver a "happy face"?

   _____

   _____

   _____

Recall details. *(Write **T** for true or **F** for false.)*

8. ____ "Expressive" cars are now available at dealerships.

9. ____ The car drives automatically if you're very angry.

10. ____ The car lights slope downward for an angry look.

11. ____ The car responds to your actions with different "looks."

12. ____ If someone cuts you off, the hood lights turn yellow.

Identify synonyms.

creation   reacts   emotions   furious

13. feelings / _____

14. invention / _____

15. angry / _____

16. responds /_____

Look it up in a reference source.

17. In what decade were airbags first commercially available?

   _____

READ: *The custom of kissing has been around for quite some time.*

SOME FACTS ABOUT KISSING

Sealed with a Kiss

If you want to be scientific, here's what happens when you kiss someone. Some 26 calories are burned in a one-minute kiss. The two people also exchange more than 250 colonies of bacteria. Luckily, most of them are beneficial.

In the Dark Ages (A.D. 476–A.D. 1000), kisses showed your social status. If you kissed people on the mouth, you were equal to them. If people were socially superior to you, you kissed them on the hand, knee, or foot. People who were *inferior* kissed *you*.

During London's Great Plague of 1665, people were afraid to greet each other with kisses. Instead, they bowed, curtsied, waved, or tipped their hats. Some of these customs still prevail in modern times.

Today, there are many different kissing customs. The normal greeting in Europe is to kiss both cheeks. Eskimos, Polynesians, and Malaysians rub noses instead of touching lips. In Hollywood, the usual greeting is to kiss the *air* beside each cheek.

Not every kiss is affectionate. In the movie, *The Godfather II,* Michael Corleone kisses his brother, who has betrayed him. But this is "the kiss of death." It means that Michael will soon have his brother killed.

REFLECT: *Think about kissing and other social customs.*

1. Name a movie that has a kissing scene, or a song that mentions kissing.

   _____

2. Name a form of greeting that's *not* mentioned in the reading.

   _____

3. Suppose a woman were introduced to the queen of England. What is the traditional way for her to greet the queen? _____

RESPOND: *Circle a letter or word, fill in the blanks, or write out the answer.*

Recall details.

1. Why were people afraid to kiss during the Great Plague?

   _____

   _____

2. During the Middle Ages, what did it mean if someone kissed your knee?

   _____

   _____

Draw conclusions.

3. During the plague, what other form of greeting did people probably avoid besides kissing?

   _____

   _____

4. Why might Hollywood "air-kissers" want to avoid kissing each other's cheeks?

   _____

   _____

Build your vocabulary.

5. In the Dark Ages, kissing was a *serious business*.

   a. People were more serious then.

   b. Kissing spread disease.

   c. A kiss had serious consequences.

6. People *exchange* bacteria during a kiss.

   a. Bacteria travel from one person's mouth to another's.

   b. Beneficial bacteria trade places during a kiss.

   c. Mouths contain enormous amounts of bacteria.

7. Kissing showed *your social status*.

   a. where you ranked compared to others

   b. whether or not you were popular

   c. how much you had to pay in taxes

8. Michael Corleone gave his brother the *kiss of death*.

   a. He gave his brother a deadly disease.

   b. He indicated that his brother would be killed.

   c. He knew he was going to die soon.

Identify antonyms. (Complete words from the reading.)

9. hostile /

   *a*_ _ _ _ _ _ _ _ _ _ _

10. superior / *i*_ _ _ _ _ _ _ _

11. rare / *u*_ _ _ _ _

12. private / *p*_ _ _ _ _ _

13. harmful / *b*_ _ _ _ _ _ _ _ _ _

Look it up in a reference source.

14. Write the dictionary definition of the word "colonies," as in *colonies of bacteria.*

    _____

    _____

    _____

    _____

    _____

READ: *How to deal with two dangerous animals.*

DANGEROUS ANIMALS

TITLE 1: _____

_____

It's true that a few mountain lions have attacked people unprovoked. Most mountain lions, however, avoid people. If you are in mountain lion habitat, don't travel alone. This is especially true at dawn or dusk. Those are the times when mountain lions are most active.

What if you *do* encounter a mountain lion? Do whatever you can to make yourself appear larger. Hold open your jacket. If children are with you, pick them up. Be loud! Wave your arms and shout. Back away slowly, but *do not run*. Running will make the mountain lion think you are prey.

If you are attacked, fight back. Most mountain lions are small enough for a human to fight. Hit the animal with stones, sticks, or fists. Blows around the eyes or mouth are most effective. Do not lie down and play dead. This makes it easier for the mountain lion to attack. Protect your neck and throat at all cost.

TITLE 2: _____

_____

The best way to protect yourself from bears is to avoid them. If you are hiking, make noise. Bears don't like surprises. If you are camping, never bring food inside your tent. If you have been cooking, change clothes.

If you're in a car, stay there—with the windows up. Bears sometimes tear cars apart if they smell food inside.

Bears are most dangerous when they're defending food or cubs. But bears that have become accustomed to eating human food are also very dangerous.

If you do encounter a bear, lie still and be quiet. Mother bears will often stop attacking if you don't fight. Don't try to climb a tree. Why? Bears can climb trees, too.

If a bear does attack—FIGHT BACK! Wave your arms. Yell and scream in a deep voice. Hit, scratch, and kick. If possible, aim for its eyes and nose.

REFLECT: *Think about other types of danger.*

1. Write an interesting title for each reading.

2. Do you think there are more dangers in a city or in the wilderness?

_____

_____

3. If you encounter a person who might hurt you, what can you do to save yourself?

_____

_____

_____

RESPOND: *Circle a letter or word, fill in the blanks, or write out the answer.*

Build your vocabulary.

1. When you stay away from people, you (attract / avoid) them.

2. The time of day when it's getting dark is called (dusk / dawn).

3. You (encounter / embrace) something when you meet with it.

4. To an animal, its food is its (habitat / prey).

Make inferences.

5. From the phrase "make yourself appear larger," you can infer that
   a. mountain lions are fairly small.
   b. bears are really large.
   c. mountain lions like big people.

6. From "don't wear clothes you've cooked in," you can infer that
   a. bears hate food smells.
   b. bears will be attracted to the smell of food.
   c. you shouldn't wear clothes when you cook.

7. From "aim for its eyes and nose," you can infer that
   a. bears have little sense of smell.
   b. bears' eyes and noses are very sensitive.
   c. blows to the face make bears angry.

8. From "protect your neck and throat at all costs," you can infer that
   a. mountain lions often attack the neck and throat.
   b. mountain lions have sensitive necks.
   c. your throat smells like food.

Make comparisons.

9. Name one behavior that's *good* advice if you meet a bear, but *bad* advice if you meet a mountain lion.

   _____
   _____

10. Name two actions that might keep you safe around bears *and* mountain lions.

    _____
    _____

Recognize synonyms.

11. ____ defend   a. daybreak
12. ____ appear   b. protect
13. ____ dawn   c. rip
14. ____ tear   d. seem

Look it up in a reference source.

15. What three steps does the American Red Cross recommend if you're bitten by a venomous snake?

    • _____
      _____
    • _____
      _____
    • _____
      _____

READ: *A waste of money or a fast track to wealth?*

THE LOTTERY

Lotteries have been around since the 1700s. In fact, the U.S. government held lotteries to help pay for the Revolutionary and Civil Wars!

States didn't hold lotteries until the 1960s. Today, 37 states rake in $17 *billion* a year from lotteries.

There are many types of legal gambling. What's legal and what isn't often depends on where you live. A legal game in one state may be illegal in another. Some common types of gambling are roulette, horse or dog racing, and slot machines.

It's easier to win at some kinds of gambling than others. But the odds of winning the lottery are lowest of all. Some 97 million people play the lottery every year. But here's how many win a million dollars—only .000008 percent!

Even if they win the lottery, some people never see the cash. In 1983, Don Temple bought a lottery ticket and won $10,000. But he'd accidentally thrown his ticket into a trash can next to the convenience store. Temple searched through the store's trash for four days, but he never did find the ticket. *And* he had to pay $200 to have the trash hauled away.

In 1985, Donna Lee Sobb won $100 in the California lottery. This qualified her for a chance at the $2 million jackpot. But when her photograph appeared in a local paper, a law officer recognized her. Donna Lee Sobb was wanted for shoplifting! Her moment of fame got her quickly arrested. Perhaps Sobb should have spent her money on a magazine instead of a lottery ticket! It would have been a better bet.

What happens if you win a $1 million lottery? Many lottery jackpots are paid in installments over 20 to 25 years. The government withholds 28 percent in taxes from each check. So at a 20-year payout, you'll receive $50,000 a year— less 28 percent tax. That leaves you with $36,000 a year. And you may also have to pay additional income taxes when you file your tax return. So don't quit your job just yet!

REFLECT: *Think about the effects of money.*

1. Suppose you won a big lottery. What would you do with the money?

   _____

   _____

2. Do you think people change if they win a lot of money? Explain your answer.

   _____

   _____

RESPOND: *Circle a letter or word, fill in the blanks, or write out the answer.*

Recall details. *(Write **T** for true or **F** for false.)*

1. ____ Some types of gambling are illegal in certain states.

2. ____ The odds of winning the lottery are very high.

3. ____ Lotteries have been used to pay for wars.

4. ____ Lotteries are just one type of gambling.

5. ____ The first lottery was held in 1983.

6. ____ Every state in the nation has a lottery.

7. ____ States started holding lotteries in the 1970s.

Draw conclusions.

8. Who makes the most money on lotteries?

   a. the federal government

   b. the states

   c. people who win

9. Your chances of winning are best in

   a. horse racing.

   b. slot machines.

   c. the lottery.

Recognize the author's tone.

10. The tone of this reading is

    a. formal and serious.

    b. scientific and scholarly.

    c. informal, conversational

Match synonyms.

garbage   celebrity   wager   picture   submit

11. bet / _____

12. file / _____

13. trash / _____

14. photograph / _____

15. fame / _____

Make a comparison.

16. Name one similarity between Don Temple's story and Donna Lee Sobb's story.

    _____

    _____

Fact or Opinion? *(Write **F** or **O**.)*

17. ____ Shoplifting is a form of stealing.

18. ____ All forms of gambling should be outlawed.

19. ____ Nearly 100 million people play the lottery every year.

20. ____ Buying lottery tickets is a waste of money.

21. ____ States have conducted lotteries for about 40 years.

22. ____ Lottery winnings are heavily taxed.

Look it up in a reference source.

23. How much is a *billion*?

    _____

READ: *Consider both sides of an argument.*

GUN-CONTROL PROPAGANDA

CITY OF XYZ BALLOT

PROPOSITION X

**MAKE OWNERSHIP OF HANDGUNS
BY PRIVATE CITIZENS ILLEGAL**

VOTE YES ON X!

Last summer, Amy Strickland was a happy little girl. At five years old, she was looking forward to her first day of school. But now she's dead. Why? She and a playmate discovered a gun in a drawer. Because too many of us keep handguns in our homes, another senseless tragedy has occurred.

Proposition X, the ban on handguns, will keep our families safe from these lethal weapons.

Handguns and families are a deadly mix. Members of every family have arguments. But too many arguments are settled "once and for all" by handguns. The result: a family torn apart—all because a handgun was readily available during the heat of an argument.

Opponents of Prop. X warn that criminals will take advantage of unarmed citizens.

Countless studies prove them wrong. *Most people killed by handguns are victims of accidents or family disputes.* Handguns belong in the hands of peace officers, not in our homes.

A vote for Prop. X will keep our families safe. Vote Yes on X.
—written by Citizens Against Handgun Violence

VOTE NO ON X!

Jeffrey Coleman would be dead if he hadn't had his handgun. Acting in self defense, he wounded the thug who threatened him. This courageous citizen dared to stand up to drug dealers in his neighborhood. Coleman is a hero. But he could have been a *dead* hero.

Take away handguns and you take away citizens' right to defend themselves. This right has been ours since the birth of our nation. Don't let Prop. X take our precious rights away!

Imagine the chaos if Prop. X passes. Imagine being alone with a criminal—with no means to defend yourself. Law-abiding citizens will be stripped of their protection. But criminals will keep their guns!

Vote to keep our city safe. Vote NO on X.
—written by the Committee for a Safe City

REFLECT: *Think about our right to vote.*

1. Many people don't bother to vote in elections. Why do you think this is so?

   _____

   _____

2. Proposition X is not real. But some cities have actually voted on whether or not to ban handguns. Would you vote to ban handguns? Why or why not?

   _____

   _____

RESPOND: *Circle a letter or word, fill in the blanks, or write out the answer.*

Build your vocabulary.

| dispute | senseless | chaos | numerous | opponent |

1. If something has no meaning, it is

   _____.

2. When everything is left to chance, the result is _____.

3. The adjective _____ means "a large number" of things.

4. A heated quarrel may also be called a _____.

5. An _____ of something is against it.

Making inferences.

6. Propaganda always *serves the author* (the person or people who wrote it). How do the two readings serve their authors?

   a. They try to inform people about handgun history.

   b. They emphasize only their own points of view.

   c. They urge people to keep and use handguns safely.

7. Propaganda tries to stir up emotions such as sympathy or anger. How does the *first* reading do that?

   a. It describes the death of a five-year-old girl.

   b. It argues that only police should have handguns.

   c. It claims that studies prove their opponents wrong.

8. Another emotion that propaganda often appeals to is *fear*. Which sentence in the *second* reading was designed to cause fear?

   a. Imagine being alone with a criminal.

   b. Don't let Prop. X take our rights away!

   c. A vote for Prop. X will keep families safe.

Fact or opinion?

Propaganda is not always factual. Write **F** or **O** for *fact* or *opinion*.

9. ____ Jeffrey Coleman would be dead if he hadn't used his handgun.

10. ____ Amy Strickland died because she found a handgun in a drawer.

11. ____ More and more criminals will take advantage of unarmed citizens.

Predicting outcomes.

12. If Prop. X becomes a law, what would happen?

    _____

    _____

13. If Prop. X fails, what would happen?

    _____

    _____

Look it up in a reference source.

14. Write the dictionary definition of *propaganda*.

    _____

    _____

    _____

    _____

READ: *In a disaster, knowledge is power!*

HOW TO SURVIVE AN EARTHQUAKE

Suppose you're standing still, but you suddenly feel as if you're moving. Then you notice that the curtains are swaying. *It's an earthquake!*

If you're inside, stay there. If you run outside, you could get hit by breaking glass or other falling objects. Get under a sturdy desk or table. (If you can, first shove the desk or table into a doorway.) Keep away from fireplaces, appliances, or heavy furniture.

If you're outside, head into the open. Stay away from buildings, power lines, big signs—or anything else that might fall on you.

What if you're in a car? Stop in a safe place. Carefully pull over to the side of the road. Stay away from trees and light posts. Don't stop under a bridge or overpass. Wait until the shaking stops before you get out of the car.

When the quake stops, deal with any injuries. If you or anyone around you is injured, apply first aid. Then try to get help. Never move a seriously injured person unless he or she is in danger. Cover the person with a blanket if you have one.

Check your home for gas leaks. If you see broken pipes or smell gas, turn off the main gas valve. If you think there might be a leak, don't use matches, lighters, appliances, or electrical equipment. They could create a spark and ignite the gas. The result could be an explosion or fire.

Be careful when you open closets and cupboards. Heavy items may have shifted during the quake. They could tumble out and fall on you as soon as the door is opened.

Beware of power lines. Don't touch any power lines that have fallen down. Also, stay away from any objects that are in contact with them.

Be prepared for aftershocks! Another quake, even a larger one, may be on its way. Aftershocks can continue for

REFLECT: *Think about nature and how it can affect us.*

1. Has the weather ever affected your life? It might have been anything from a flooded home to a rained-out baseball game. Write a short description of the event.

_____

_____

_____

_____

2. Suppose a natural disaster (earthquake, tornado, flood, etc.) forced you to leave your home. List six things you would take with you to survive the next few days.

- _____   • _____   • _____
- _____   • _____   • _____

RESPOND: *Circle a letter or word, fill in the blanks, or write out the answer.*

Build your vocabulary.

1. To *come in contact with* something is to (avoid / touch) it.

2. During a quake, objects may have *shifted* (moved / stayed put).

3. If you *deal with* something, you (handle it / avoid it).

4. Something that *sways* moves (back and forth / up and down).

5. Something that *ignites* (loses power / catches on fire).

Draw conclusions. *(More than one answer may be correct.)*

6. Why is the kitchen a dangerous place to be during an earthquake?
   a. Kitchen appliances could tip over and injure you.
   b. Broken gas lines could cause dangerous leaks.
   c. Objects could tumble from overhead cupboards.

7. Imagine being in the mountains when a quake hits. What dangers could you face?
   a. becoming confused and losing your memory
   b. getting hit by falling rocks and trees
   c. none; mountains are safe in a quake

8. If you are near a window when an earthquake hits, what should you do?
   a. Stay near the window so you can jump out quickly.
   b. Look out the window so you can see what's going on.
   c. Get away from the window since it might break and shower you with glass.

9. Why is a doorway a good place to stand during an earthquake?
   a. You can get outside quickly from there.
   b. Doorways are sturdy and will protect you.
   c. You'll be able to answer the door if someone knocks.

10. Why could it be dangerous to stand near a chimney?
    a. You could be hit by falling bricks or stones.
    b. There is no danger. It's completely safe to stand near a chimney.
    c. The only danger is getting dirty from ashes.

Look it up in a reference source.

11. The San Francisco earthquake of 1906 is often called "the big one." What was its approximate rating on the Richter scale?

_____

READ: *Some little-known facts about a well-known president.*

ANOTHER LOOK AT ABE LINCOLN

Abraham Lincoln is one of our best-loved presidents. But how much do we really know about him? Most people don't realize that he ran for office many times—and lost.

Lincoln was defeated when he ran for the Illinois legislature. He was finally elected to that legislature in 1834. Then he tried to become speaker of the house. But, again, he lost—twice. He also lost the race for the U.S. Senate—twice. He tried to be nominated for vice president, but failed.

In 1860, Lincoln ran for president, and won. He was re-elected in 1864.

We think of Lincoln as an unusually honest man. But the same cannot be said for some of his supporters. They weren't above a dirty trick or two.

In 1860, the Republicans held their national convention. Their purpose was to nominate a candidate to run for president against the Democrats. Lincoln's supporters forged passes to that convention. A great many of them were able to get in. The unfair result was that hundreds of people who supported *other* candidates were shut out! Lincoln won the nomination and went on to become president.

The Lincoln we see in the movies has a fine, deep voice. But Lincoln's actual voice was high-pitched, piercing, and a bit shrill. In those days without microphones, he was probably easy to hear.

When we think of Lincoln, we often think of his famous "Gettysburg Address." Many people believe it is one of the finest speeches ever made. But at the time it was given, some people hated it. A *Chicago Times* reporter wrote that the speech was "an embarrassment to every American."

REFLECT: *What do you know about Abraham Lincoln?*

Circle three letters.

a. Lincoln was very hard of hearing.

b. Lincoln gave the Gettysburg Address.

c. Lincoln grew up in California.

d. He kept many pets in the White House.

e. He was president during America's Civil War.

f. Lincoln was assassinated while watching a play.

g. Lincoln was president during WW II.

h. Lincoln was afraid of electricity.

RESPOND: *Circle a letter or word, fill in the blanks, or write out the answer.*

Build your vocabulary.

nominate	piercing	forge	legislature	address

1. The group of people who has the power to make laws is called the _____.

2. To _____ someone is to choose them as a candidate to run for office.

3. A sound that seems to go right through your head is

   _____.

4. To _____ something is to copy it in order to cheat or trick people.

5. The words _____ and *speech* are synonyms.

Recall details. *(More than one answer may be correct.)*

6. If you are a member of the Utah legislature, you make laws for the residents of
   a. the nation.
   b. one state.
   c. Chicago.

7. The presidential nominee of the Democratic Party runs against a
   a. Senator.
   b. Democrat.
   c. Republican.

8. Lincoln lost when he ran for
   a. U.S. Senator.
   b. vice president.
   c. mayor.

9. Lincoln's supporters forged passes to
   a. the Republican Convention.
   b. the Democratic Convention.
   c. the state legislature.

Draw conclusions. *(More than one answer may be correct.)*

10. If Lincoln's supporters hadn't packed the convention,
    a. Lincoln might not have become president.
    b. Lincoln might have never been a senator.
    c. Lincoln might not have been a war president.

11. Regarding the Gettysburg Address, we can assume that
    a. the *Chicago Times* hated Lincoln.
    b. many senators didn't like the speech.
    c. most people didn't agree with the *Chicago Times*.

Look it up in a reference source.

12. Write the first six words of the Gettysburg Address.

    _____

    _____

READ: *The Olympics are about much more than sports.*

THE OLYMPICS: MIRROR OF THE WORLD

It was 1896 when the first modern games were held in Greece. There were 311 competitors—all men—from 13 countries. Most of the non-Greek competitors were college students on summer vacation.

Since then, the Olympic Games have become more complicated. They have been a battleground for disputes between nations. Sometimes they've been unfair. For years, the Olympics discriminated against women and enabled only wealthy men to participate. And in spite of testing, drug use has now cast a long shadow over the games. Every year, the games seem to grow more commerical. Over time, the Olympics have held a mirror to our world—reflecting its problems, and sometimes, its progress.

In the 1900 games, women were allowed to participate for the first time. But they could only compete in long skirts. For years, it was thought that running was too strenuous for women. But as the world slowly changed, so did the games. Gradually, more and more events became open to women.

The Olympics also banned professional athletes. Only amateur athletes could compete—in other words, only those who could afford to pay for their own training. Nations found ways to get around this. Countries such as Russia simply gave money to their amateur athletes. Often they were paid for jobs they never performed. The United States also supported athletes in the form of athletic scholarships.

Friction between some nations darkened many of the games. In 1936, Germany hosted the Olympics. The U.S. almost boycotted the games to protest Hitler's anti-Jewish policies. But in the end, the U.S. decided to participate. Several African-Americans, including the great Jesse Owens, won medals. But Hitler refused to recognize them. He hated not only Jews, but blacks, too.

Because of World War II, the games were not held in 1940 and 1944. They began again in 1948.

In 1960, the games were shown on television for the first time. Suddenly the Olympics had an audience of a couple of billion people. So a protest by U.S. sprinters Tommy Smith and John Carlos was seen all over the world. As they were about to receive their medals, they raised their fists in the air. This was meant to protest U. S. racial policies.

In 1972, the world witnessed an Olympic tragedy. Palestinian terrorists kidnapped 11 Israeli athletes. The police attacked when they tried to escape with their hostages. At the end of the battle, every Israeli athlete was dead, along with three terrorists. Yet in spite of some protests, the 1972 games went on as scheduled.

In 1980, the U.S. boycotted the games. This was to protest Russia's invasion of Afghanistan. Sixty-one other countries also joined the boycott. Not surprisingly, Russia won the most medals that year.

In 1984, rules about commercializing the games were relaxed. The five-ring Olympic logo quickly appeared on everything from soda cans to tires.

In 1988, professional athletes were finally welcomed to the games. But that year the Olympics also saw its first drug scandal. Ten athletes were disqualified after testing positive for drug use. One was Ben Johnson, a Canadian sprinter, who was stripped of his gold medal. For 16 years, Olympic officials had randomly tested athletes for drug use. But finding absolute proof of drug use is extremely difficult.

In 1992, the sun shone on the Olympics. For once there was no friction between the countries. And South Africa was welcomed back to the games. For years, that country had been banned for excluding blacks from its teams. But in 1992, South Africa competed with a multiracial team.

The next Olympics will be held in Beijing, China, in 2008. Who knows what sort of changes we'll be likely to see?

BEIJING 2008

REFLECT: *Think about sports in our country.*

1. The Olympic Games are an *international* event.
   Name one *national* sports event in the United States. _____

2. Do you think athletes should be allowed to use performance-enhancing drugs?
   Why or why not? _____
   _____
   _____

3. What do you like best about watching a sport on TV? _____
   _____

   What do you like best about watching a sport live? _____
   _____

4. Name your favorite sport to play or watch. Why do you prefer it to any other?
   Or, if you don't like sports, explain why. _____
   _____

RESPOND: *Circle a letter or word, fill in the blanks, or write out the answer.*

Identify the main idea.

1. Which sentence sums up the main idea of the reading?
   a. The Olympics have been full of conflict.
   b. The Olympics reflect the world's history.
   c. We need to do away with the Olympics.

Build your vocabulary.

2. When people on different teams *compete*, they
   a. strive against each other for a prize.
   b. join others in a great celebration.
   c. try to make the other team look bad.

3. *Amateurs* compete in a sport
   a. only if they're paid for it.
   b. for pleasure, rather than money.
   c. if they've had training.

4. A sporting event becomes *commercial* when it is
   a. paid for by advertisers.
   b. cheered by the audience.
   c. shown on television.

5. If you *boycott* an event, you
   a. send young boys to compete.
   b. try to win more medals than anyone else.
   c. stay away to show your disapproval.

6. There is *friction* between nations that
   a. compete.   b. disagree.   c. protest.

7. A *strenuous* race
   a. is exhausting for runners.
   b. attracts few participants.
   c. is boring to watch.

Recall details.

8. All athletes in the 1896 Olympics were (amateurs / professionals).

9. Before 1998, the United States gave its athletes (scholarships / low-paying jobs).

10. The Olympics once (excluded / welcomed) South Africa for banning black athletes.

11. In 1984, the games became more (competitive / commercialized).

12. Television brought the games to (millions / billions) of people.

13. In the 1936 games, Hitler refused to recognize (South African / African-American) winners.

Draw conclusions.

14. After 11 Israeli athletes were killed, the 1972 games went on in spite of protests. Why were there protests?

    _____

    _____

    _____

    _____

    _____

15. For years, only amateurs could compete in the games. Why was this unfair to poor athletes?

_____

_____

_____

_____

16. Think about what happened in previous games. Then think about conflict between nations today. What could possibly happen in Beijing? More than one answer is correct.

   a. Women could be excluded from competing.

   b. Terrorists could disrupt the games.

   c. Jews could be excluded from the games.

   d. One or several countries could boycott the games.

   e. Some athletes could protest at the games.

   f. Only amateur athletes could participate.

Interpret figurative language.

17. Drug use *cast a long shadow* over the games.

   a. made the games seem dim and dark

   b. was a problem from the beginning

   c. recently became a troubling problem

18. The Olympics have *held a mirror to our world*.

   a. reflected our world

   b. brightened our world

   c. held our world high

Compare and contrast.

19. List two major differences between the 1988 Olympics and the 1896 games.

   • _____

   _____

   • _____

   _____

Put details in order.

20. Number the events to show the order in which they happened.

   _____ South Africa was welcomed back to the games.

   _____ Palestinian terrorists kidnapped 11 Israeli athletes.

   _____ Women were allowed to compete in the games.

   _____ The Olympics were first broadcast on television.

   _____ The United States boycotted the Olympics.

Look it up in a reference source.

21. Write three facts about any one of the following:

   • the International Olympic Committee
   • the Olympic games in ancient times
   • famous Olympic athletes

   • _____

   _____

   • _____

   _____

   • _____

   _____

SADDLEBACK
EDUCATIONAL PUBLISHING

MORE EXCITING TITLES

SADDLEBACK'S "IN CONTEXT" SERIES
(Six 112-page worktexts in each series)
- English
- Vocabulary
- Reading
- Practical Math

SADDLEBACK'S "SKILLS AND STRATEGIES" SERIES
(Six 144-page reproducible workbooks in each series)
- Building Vocabulary
- Language Arts
- Math Computation
- Reading Comprehension

READING COMPREHENSION SKILL BOOSTERS
- Read-Reflect-Respond, Books A, B, C, & D

WRITING 4
(Four 64-page worktexts)
- Descriptive Writing
- Expository Writing
- Narrative Writing
- Persuasive Writing

CURRICULUM BINDERS
(100+ activities in each binder)

ENGLISH, READING, WRITING . . .
- Beginning Writing 1 & 2
- Writing 1 & 2
- Good Grammar
- Language Arts 1 & 2
- Reading for Information 1 & 2
- Reading Comprehension 1 & 2
- Spelling Steps 1, 2, 3, & 4
- Survival Vocabulary 1 & 2

MATHEMATICS . . .
- Pre-Algebra
- Algebra 1 & 2
- Geometry

SCIENCE . . .
- Earth, Life, & Physical

STUDY SKILLS & TEST PREP . . .
- Standardized Test Prep 1 & 2
- Study Skills 1 & 2

SADDLEBACK'S HIGH-INTEREST READING SERIES
- Astonishing Headlines
- Barclay Family Adventures
- Carter High
- Disasters
- Illustrated Classics Series
- Life of...Series
- PageTurners
- Quickreads
- Strange But True Stories
- Saddleback's Classics
- Walker High

Visit us at www.sdlback.com for even more Saddleback titles.